RAINY DAY

SAFETY & ELOPEMENT SUPPORT

EmpowerED Autism

This book is intended as an educational resource and is not a substitute for professional advice or supervision.

Printed in the United States of America.

How to use this book:

- Look at the pictures
- Talk about safe choices
- Circle, check or color
- Practice together

This book helps children practice safe choices during rainy days.

Key Safety Language and Consistency

Children benefit from clear, consistent language across home, school, and community settings. When discussing safety during rainy days or times of increased elopement risk, using the same simple phrases can support understanding and regulation.

Recommended Safety Language:

"Stay inside"
"Wait"
"Door stays closed"
"Stay with an adult"
"We are safe inside"

Rainy Day Sequence

1. **The rain starts**
2. **The door stays closed**
3. **Kai is by the window**
4. **Dad comes to join him**
5. **They relax and read a book**

Safety Scenarios

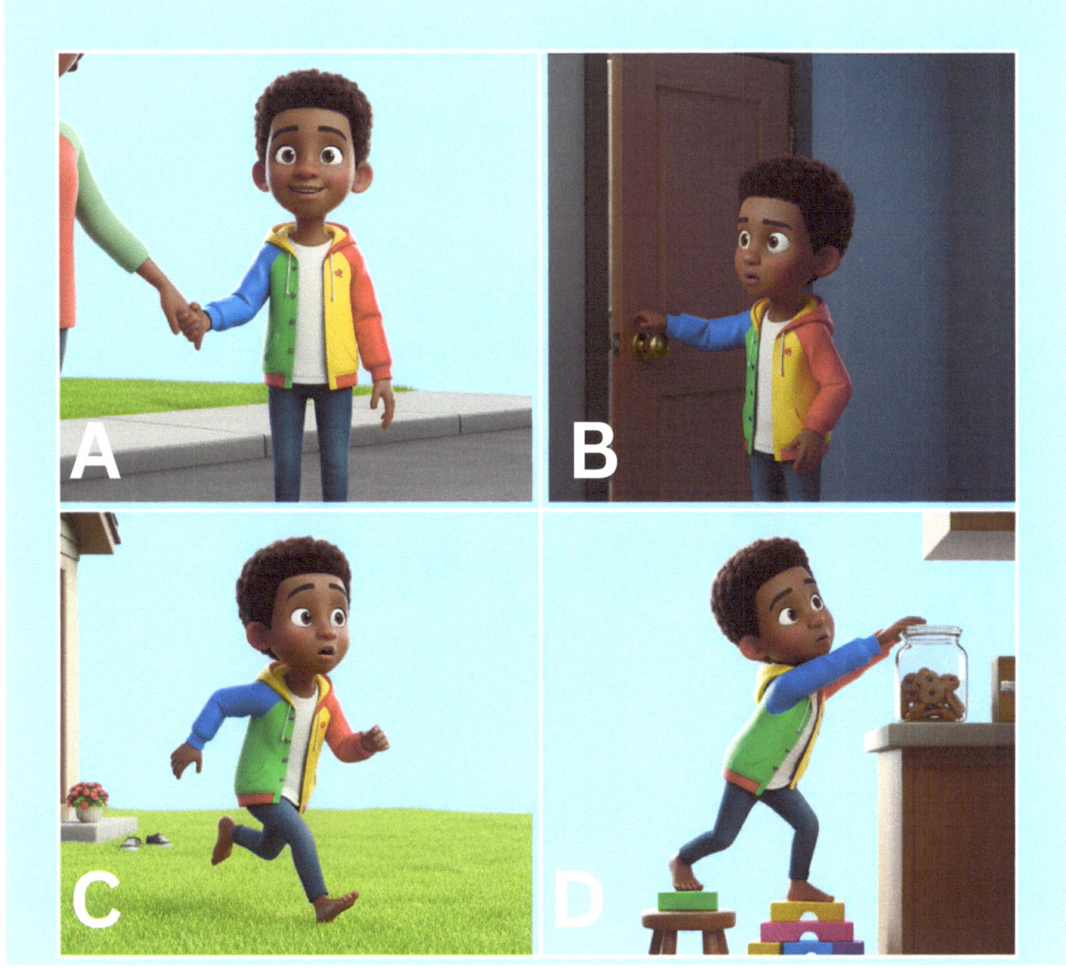

Which action is safe? Point to or circle it:

A. Holding an adults hand
B. Opening a door without an adult
C. Running outside with no shoes on
D. Standing on items to reach cookies

Staying Safe on a Rainy Day

Checklist:

- [ ] Stay inside
- [ ] Stay with an adult
- [ ] Holds hands
- [ ] Stop and wait

Stop & Choose

Elopement Focus

Select the Safest Scenario:

- Running alone outside
- Staying inside with an adult

☐ ☐

Rainy Day Safety Check

Yes or No

Is it safe to stay inside when it's raining?

○ Yes ○ No

Is it safe to open doors alone?

○ Yes ○ No

When outside, should you hold an adult's hand?

○ Yes ○ No

Practice Waiting

Kai really wants to go outside. Should he wait for an adult or go outside alone?

○ **Wait**

○ **Go**

Indoor Activities

Safe indoor activities when it's raining outside:

Read a book, build blocks, play with an adult, or color

Rainy Day Body Rules

If outside:

- [ ] Wear a raincoat

- [ ] Hands stay with adult

- [ ] Body stays calm

- [ ] Wait before moving

Micro Social Story

It is raining.
Kai stays inside.
Kai waits and plays with toys.
Kai is safe.

Take a deep breath while you color

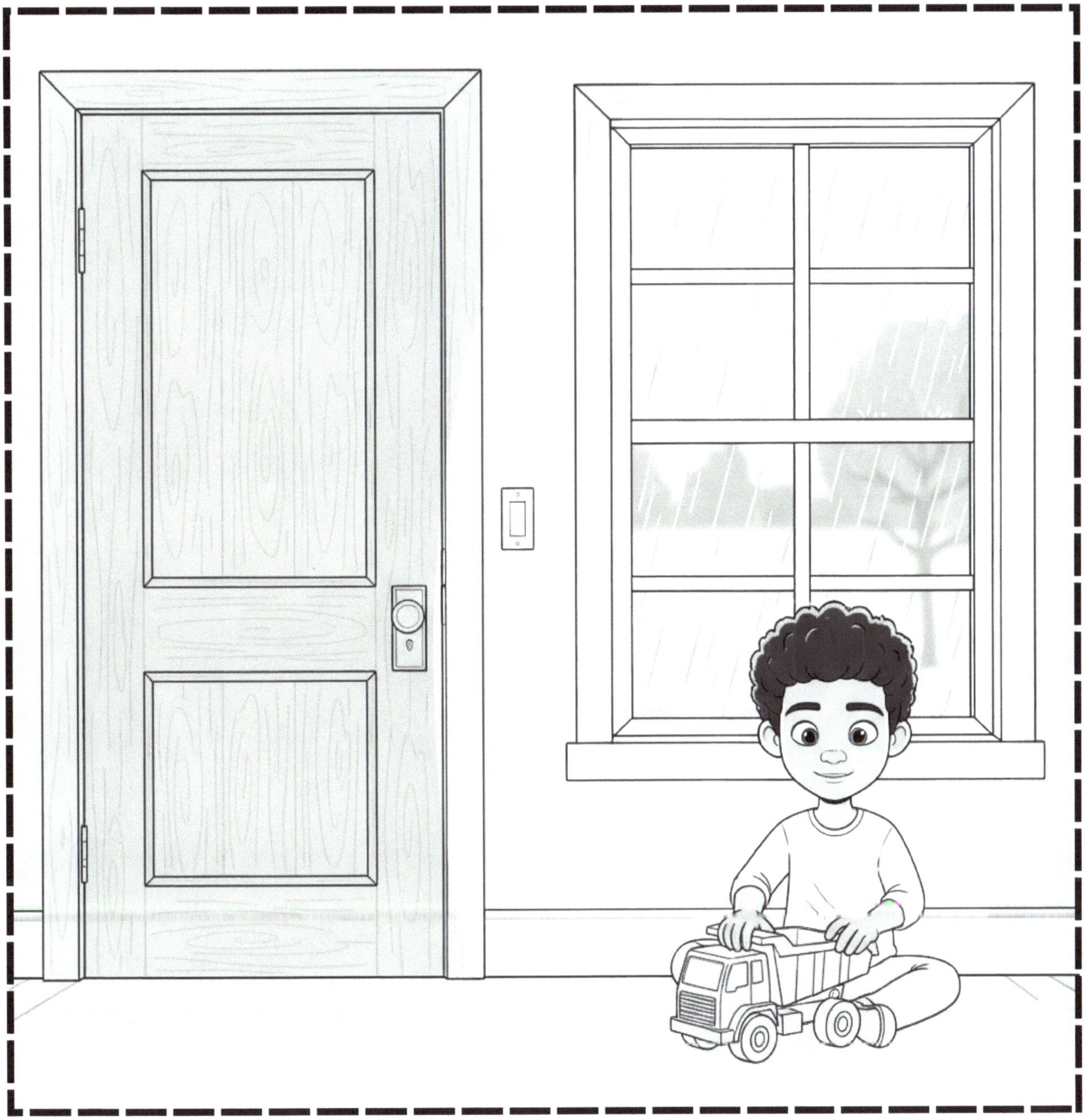

Communication Skills

Circle Trusted Adults

Communication Skills

I Can Say This:

- [ ] My name is ________________.
- [ ] I need help.
- [ ] Please call my adult.

Family

Draw your family:

Identification & Awareness

About Me Page (safety info)

- Name:
- Age:
- Phone number:

Emotional Regulation

My Calm Plan Checklist:

- [ ] Breathe
- [ ] Ask for help
- [ ] Use comfort item

- [ ] Go to safe space

Emotional Regulation

Feelings & Body Signals

Sometimes I want to wander when I feel:

- ○ Tired
- ○ Overwhelmed
- ○ Excited
- ○ Curious

Practice & Reinforcement

My Safety Promise (choose your why)

I will stay with my trusted adults because:

- ◯ My adults keep me safe
- ◯ I don't want to get lost
- ◯ I want help to find me quickly if I need it
- ◯ Safety helps me feel calm and strong

For Caregivers & Educators

Create a village

Medical ID bracelet

Family photo

This activity book is designed to reinforce safety concepts introduced in *Kai's Rainy Day Adventure*, including ID supports and family safety planning

Closing Note

This resource handbook was created to support caregivers, educators, and professionals as they guide children through everyday safety situations, including increased elopement risk during rainy days.

The strategies and examples included are intended to complement existing support systems, and to encourage consistent, calm responses across home, school, and community settings. Each child's needs and circumstances are unique, and this resource is designed to be adapted as needed.

Thank you for the work you do each day to support safety, understanding, and well-being.

Maryse Alexander